"Jessica has the rare gift of being able to connect directly to the mind, body and soul through both her therapeutic work and her writing.

This book is a guide for learning how to slow your mind and body down enough to listen to your 'gut' and to realize the universe's true plan for you.

She combines her wisdom, examples as well as clear Action Steps to lay out a path for finding our way through this complicated human existence."

Sarah Allen Benton, MS, LMHC, LPC, AADC

*Therapist and author of*
Understanding the High-Functioning Alcoholic

# Acknowledgements

To my family and friends:

It is because of all of you that I have learned what unconditional love is. What it means to go through amazing and challenging times with love that never waivers. It is this unconditional love that all of you provide that allows me to be who I am. To take risks and show my sass without fear, because I know I always have you in my corner to come back to. I also want to thank you for always supporting my ideas, no matter how far-fetched they may seem. Knowing you're all behind me gives me the courage to step outside of my comfort zone to challenge myself. These are just a few of the many gifts you have given me that I will never forget. I will be forever grateful to you.

To my team of colleagues:

I could never be where I am without the support of everyone I have worked with throughout the years. Thank you for the opportunities, collaborative problem-solving, and creative vision. It is because you had faith in me to take on inspiring new challenges that I was able to write this book.

Let the journey continue . . .

# Introduction

## *My Beliefs and Values*

I have engaged in therapy in one way, shape, or form at different points in my life for different reasons and with different people. I thank my mother for this. It was because she presented the option to me in middle school that I was willing to try therapy. Of course, this was after I thought aloud, "If people find out, they will think I'm crazy!" Once I got over myself and realized it would be a safe space for me to just be me and receive healthy feedback from an unbiased party, I was all in.

I still seek out therapy whenever I need it. I believe that I do not have the right to sit across from someone if I am not actively able to look at who I am, and what I stand for. That's not to say I spend every day of my life analyzing everything I have said and done; I would lose my mind!

I believe very strongly that different people come into our lives for a multitude of reasons, until we die.

I also believe that people, at their core, genuinely want to be good and willing to accept the love and support that others show them along the way. They simply need to see the world through light and not through the darkness they may have experienced. In a time where the concept of resilience has been beaten to death, I believe that everyone needs a safe space to just "be" with no judgment. This is somewhat rare in a society where we are consistently judged—whether it's for what we wear, the color of our skin, our profession, the size of our house, or our bank account.

I see the therapeutic space as a safe place where people get to be, feel, and say whatever they want. Once they feel safe, they are given the opportunity to authentically work on change. When we feel safe physically and emotionally, we are willing to try new and scary things. When someone has our back, we are also more willing to take risks that we may otherwise not be willing to take. This is the beauty of the therapeutic relationship. How powerful is that?

This reassurance of safety can transmute our family relationships, our marriages, and our friendships.

The reality is that as we grow and change, the world around us changes as well. That's something we need to be aware of—and be willing to risk. As we "choose us" and choose growth, people may or may not continue to walk beside us due to the uncertainty they feel about "where we are going" or who we have become. When we make changes in our lives, it is essential that we allow things to unfold, organically. For many of us, that statement alone is angst-provoking. I get it. However, the more we try to control the outcome, the more we fight the natural flow of finding our purpose. That is a mistake. It's like pushing a huge boulder up a hill and wondering why you can't breathe. Believe me, I have done it myself.

This leads us to the value of letting go, literally, figuratively, and metaphorically. Letting go is not an easy feat, yet people talk about it as if it's the most effortless thing in the world. The truth is that most people who say they have "let it go" hold onto these emotions or situations in their bodies for a very long time and it eats away at them.

There are two phases of letting go: the emotional release and the physical release that follows. You may feel most comfortable discharging emotion verbally with a trusted loved one—or physically through exercise. Yet the most effective route to let go of something is both emotional and physical. This is where my work as a therapist and Reiki master comes into play.

In general, it is much easier to focus on letting go of what is easiest for us at any particular juncture. My husband and I often talk about the way many people tend to gravitate toward growth in the area that feels most manageable to them. This makes sense—and it's a great way to keep up the momentum as you make progress.

However, there comes a time when we need to do the dreaded stepping outside of our comfort zone. In that moment, we begin to heal the part of us that we have kept in the dark for a long time—and it takes an intense wrenching from our reserves of strength to stay the course. It is also the point at which we begin to address where our emotions sit in our body and truly understand how it feels to finally and completely let go.

One of the many things I love about my work is giving people the opportunity to "speak their need" the minute they walk through my door. It is within that instant when they choose therapy or Reiki that I ask them to begin the practice of identifying their need. It is a beautiful moment when they express what they want—and when that need is met. It is a feeling that is very powerful and yet particularly unfamiliar to most of us.

There is such a thing as not having much to say, and there is such a thing as too much therapy. I also believe that it is possible to become "talked out," which is exactly why I went on to train as a

Reiki practitioner. I believe a goal of therapy is to get people back into their hearts and bodies, and out of their heads. How can we expect a miracle to take place when we constantly engage in an activity that reinforces overthinking or overanalyzing?

In my practice, as we shift between Reiki and therapy, my clients could venture into the unknown (their bodies) as they trust their intuition and move forward when they are ready and feel it's right. You can't make someone see something they aren't ready to see.

However, by giving people the opportunity to decide what treatment they would like in that moment, they are able to explore the unknown parts of themselves in a gentle and calming way. It allows them to be truly open for a period of time and to explore the therapy of their choice. It is pure perfection, as when they can choose the treatment modality, they are more emotionally invested and their tolerance to change increases.

When you are on your path of growth, the universe will tempt you with your past to see how committed you are to moving forward. I see this happen repeatedly in my practice and in my own life. As the individuals I work with start to shift, there are these irksome situations that present themselves to "tempt" them to return to their comfort zone. Part of the beauty of therapy is that when a client brings this information into the room, we are able to identify the growth opportunities together.

The easiest way to illustrate what I am referring to is when someone says, "That's it, I can't take this relationship anymore. This person is not my forever and I don't know why I am staying with them."

As we work through the situation and my client decides to leave the relationship, one of the following situations may occur: the decision may have been made to end the relationship when their ex-partner calls them, begging for reconciliation, or when they meet someone new, who just happens to share many of the same qualities of their ex. They acknowledge that this person is unhealthy for them, but they may also be struggling with the grief process and feel compelled to revert back to the way it was before—even within the structure of a new, yet similar, relationship.

Each of these examples demonstrates how the universe, God—or whichever higher power you believe in—is giving you the opportunity to remain uncomfortable in order to grow through the pain, instead of retreating from it.

All too often, we hear the phrase "lean into your emotions." Let's be honest, that can be overwhelming. Emotions and behaviors are on a spectrum. There are times when we need to "sit in our feels," and that's okay.

It is up to us to take an honest look at how long is too long to sit in our emotions—and at what point the process becomes a pity party. Everyone's process varies wildly, and that understanding is at the root of the therapeutic process.

I believe we need to show respect for the changes people are going through by being their biggest cheerleader.

As a therapist, I don't determine someone's rate of change—ever! We all need someone in our corner and someone to point out the strides we are making no matter how big or small. What we focus on grows—and I point out the growth I see in clients on a regular basis to help them observe how the shifts they are choosing to make are showing up in their lives. Change is difficult for most people. But by taking a step back and getting clarity about who we are and where we are going, we can facilitate a mindset shift that makes room for growth and peace of mind.

# Chapter One

There are times in our lives when we need to take a step back and evaluate what we're doing, how we're living, and how we feel about things. It may be brought on by a life crisis or major event, such as the death of a loved one, divorce, or changing careers. It is in these times that it is very hard for us to see the macro view; to step outside of ourselves and realize what is going on. The same concept can be seen in our busy, daily lives. We can easily get caught up with work, family, and friends and cruise along on autopilot. Whether we're in the day-to-day, the moment of crisis, or a life-changing experience, we may come face-to-face with our blind spots. Our blind spots can rear their ugly head as thoughts and/or behaviors that we engage in on a regular basis, causing seemingly minor issues. However, it's not something that would stop us in our tracks. Typically, it takes a major event or crisis to unearth that blind spot so we can explore it further. These moments offer a bird's-eye view into the life we're living.

Whatever it may be, these moments create space for awareness and tuning in to ourselves. In addition, the high-level perspective permits us to do a gut check and tap into our intuition. Once connected to the inner voice and innate understanding, we are guided to a deeper sense of self and purpose. It is here that we embark on a more expansive journey. It is also from this place that we can transcend past pain and effectively shift thoughts and behaviors in our lives that no longer serve us.

## *Birthing Our Intuition*

Whether you are a parent, wish to become one, or have no intention to become a parent, the experience of giving birth is an interesting concept to ponder when looking at ourselves and our psychological well-being. Of course, we all come from parents as well, and I'm sure many would agree with what I've observed.

One of the greatest joys is watching a child be born into this world with such purity. When we see the child for the first time, there are so many thoughts that run through the mind . . . *Am I going to be a good parent? How am I going to do this? What if I screw this up?* It's in that moment that we realize the influence that we have over another life and the immeasurable goal that we have of helping shape this new life. So what do we do with this incalculable influence that we have over another human being? It is in the nine months parents have to prepare for the birth of their child that each individual takes time to reflect on who they are and what they plan to offer the life that they are bringing into this world. It is through this reflection that they think about how they were raised, what they respect about their own parents, and which things they would like to do differently. They are also required to look at the challenges they have faced and emotional baggage they carry, in order to truly assess their ability to stop the process of generational trauma. Throughout this time of contemplation, their critical responsibility is to consider their wounds—and how they can prevent these unhealed aspects of themselves from impacting their children. Child-rearing is challenging. Hence, it is important to connect with ourselves before embarking on this journey. This is where the reconnection with our gut instinct and our intuition comes into play.

### *Self-Care as a Path to Intuition: What Do I Need?*

As children, we take on our parents' beliefs, behaviors, challenges, and emotions. It is through attachment in these early years that we either learn healthy ways to access our intuition or unhealthy ways to ignore it due to our unmet needs. As we age into young adults, our intuition requires us to learn to care for ourselves by listening to our bodies and finding ways to meet our needs. To "hear" what it is we want, we must practice the art of listening. This includes listening to our own needs. As cliché as it may sound, the first step in meeting our needs is to figure out what they are. This can be done through sharing and confiding in a therapist, a trusted friend, or your partner. I often tell my clients to start their morning each day by asking themselves this question: "What do I need today?" This can be as simple as, "I need to eat breakfast before I leave the house," or "I will make sure I have a thirty-minute nap." Then check in with yourself at night before you go to sleep to see if your need was met.

How can we get angry with others for not meeting our needs when we don't even know what they are? This is all about practice on a daily basis. It's like anything else; it takes an average of sixty-five to seventy days (about two and a half months) of consistency to solidify a newly formed habit until it becomes "automatic."

The other important piece of this practice is learning how to meet our own needs so we aren't dependent upon others. So when your partner or friend looks at you in a situation and says, "What do you need?" you are able to answer them—even if the answer is, "I don't know." If you are able, try to talk through it. You may discover your need in that precise moment.

Another way to help you determine and understand your needs is to think about the things that make you feel good or inspire you. I'm referring to situations wherein you leave the activity—or the person—and you feel good. When you are able to identify the things that make you feel like they support who you are—and who you want to become—then you have found the things that you need and should strive to do more often.

These are the things that fill our soul when we are feeling depleted or empty. By engaging in these things and "feeling the good feels," we can further reveal what we need—and don't need. The more we fill ourselves up, the more summarily we are able to determine when we are depleted and need to fill up the tank, once more.

Consistent discussions with ourselves or others allow us to look at patterns we have developed throughout our lives that have impacted our belief systems. By examining these patterns, we are able to see cause-and-effect as to how our thinking impacts our behavior. It starts with simple questions such as: *What am I doing today? What do I need to feel nourished? How will I apply this wisdom going forward?*

If we don't take time to think about our needs, when will our needs ever be met? We are our truth; we are intuition. And yet, we are born into this world relying on others—such as our parents—to meet our needs. As adults, we are given the choice of reflection, awareness, and action to determine our path of growth.

As we all know, awareness is the first step to insight. But as clearly stated, it's the first step. Next, action is required. The ability to put our awareness into behavior can feel daunting at times when faced with the juggling act of being a partner, child, sibling, boss, and friend. But it is possible. Getting quiet goes a long way. When we can relinquish the role we're fulfilling for others and determine our own desires and meaning, we start to shift. What's more, we move from externally driven behaviors to internally driven ones. This is empowerment.

***What first step are you willing to take to meet your needs? What does that look like?***

## *Our Awareness and How to Access It*

Awareness begins in our body. This is the first way we become conscious of the fact that something is "off." Tune into your body. When taking a walk, do you feel your breath, your legs, and your heartbeat? Start with something you do every day. Once you become aware of these sensations, take it to the next level—perhaps when you are nervous. Stop and say to yourself, "Where do I feel this in my body?" For instance, maybe you know your boss is a trigger for you. That's the perfect time to check into your body and see where it's reacting or holding your emotions. This is important, as it allows you to connect with your body. That way, down the line when something comes up, you are able to feel it by connecting with that same physical trigger. Your body will tell you something, and you'll be able to sense it. You can take a moment and get clarity on what you're feeling.

The final step in this exercise is to communicate your feelings to others. You can say something like, "I'm struggling with something and I need to regroup. Let's revisit this next week." Clarity comes from being alone and giving yourself the space and permission to consider what's really going on. I like to call this "the pause." That is the time that your gut instinct is able to speak to you—because it can be "heard."

*When was the last time you took five minutes to sit quietly and feel what's going on in your body? Take five minutes alone today and write down what you feel in your body and what you think it's trying to communicate to you.*

# Chapter Two

## THE PAUSE

Learning to properly implement the pause can be challenging and takes regular, intentional practice. The pause is basically a way for you to stop yourself before you say or do something you may regret at a later date—and can't take back. The pause works beautifully in any and all situations we encounter that are triggering. So how do we do it? Once more, it starts with listening to your body.

Our bodies will tell us what emotion we are experiencing long before our brain can catch up. For me, when I am anxious, my belly turns and I feel sick. When I am angry, I get cold and start to shake. I know this from years of tuning in and paying attention to what my body is doing when I am having a specific emotion. In the beginning of this practice, odds are you won't notice in the moment. So what I want you to do is this: after an intense situation that has triggered any emotion, write down what it was and how your body feels. Typically, in the beginning, the correlations take place after the situation has already occurred— and that is OK. The purpose of this is for you to continue to document and be aware of the different emotions you experience and the reaction your body has to each of these emotions. As the saying goes, "What we focus on grows," and so you will grow your ability to create these connections for your "future pause."

The next step in implementing the pause can be practicing with your partner or spouse, ideally someone you live with and are close to.

Ask them to use a code word that you both agree upon to stop you in your tracks, so you pause in that moment. For example, you both know there is a certain hot topic that gets heated, more often than not. So you ask your partner to use the predetermined code word you agreed upon when they see you shaking because you are angry. This is another layer in helping you to stop, drop, and roll with an argument in a different way. It allows that split second interval to say, "Oh shit, he's right—I'm pissed. My body is shaking and I need a pause before I poke his eyeballs out."

As you practice this awareness, and you utilize the help of your partner or a couple's therapist, you will soon be able to see where you no longer need external cues because you have practiced enough that you can internally autocorrect when needed. Of course, that is not all that needs to be done when you use your pause appropriately.

What happens next is the most important piece. The pause is only as effective as your ability to circle back to the discussion calmly within a twenty-four-to-forty-eight-hour period.

This circle back is essential to your ability to move forward with someone after being triggered. It's the perfect time to express yourself in a thoughtful way, and then give the other person the same opportunity. You can then move forward in your relationship with a better understanding of what happened, and discuss the core of it, as opposed to the superficial topics that become the point of focus. Lastly, the circle back is key in order to "own" our part and uncover our triggers. It also serves to help our loved one (friend or family) better understand our "why," thereby giving context to our behavior. This perspective can also help our loved ones to recognize when it's not personal.

***What triggers you so much that you react instantly? Take some time to write down your triggers, your reactions, and how they may be harmful to your relationships.***

## *Relationship with Self*

How mind blowing it is that when we become frustrated with others, something in them is reminding us of an aspect of ourselves we struggle with. This has been said many times and in many ways, but it continues to be a difficult concept to grasp. We consistently hear about how we need to control our reactions, as that's all we have control over. Of course this is true, but don't we need to understand where the reaction is emerging from in order to figure out how to tame it?

It is also key to understand that what triggers us about someone isn't necessarily the exact thing we don't like about ourselves: it may be a variation of sorts.

The ability to do this requires us to look at who we are as a whole, not as fragmented parts. It is the sum of all these parts that makes us the whole of who we are. And yet we spend so much time trying to ignore—or avoid—the parts of ourselves we don't deem acceptable.

In my work, I have seen how we fight to block the parts of ourselves that lie in the darkest corners, covered in cobwebs. We spend more energy on covering them up than focusing on the parts of ourselves that are beautiful. By exerting this energy, we slowly lead ourselves into a rabbit hole of sadness and anxiety. We work so hard to push parts of ourself away, and it just ups the emotional and physical ante, until we see it and are willing to sit with it. What would it be like if we brought these parts into the light instead of shunning them back into the shadows? Isn't that what people yearn for on some level—to be seen? To be clear, being seen doesn't mean being famous. It means feeling like we matter, purely for who we are, not what we do, for our caretaking ability, or our money.

This then begs the question: How can we be seen if we spend so much energy hiding from ourselves? What are we hiding from? Disappointment? Disapproval? Shame? It is our responsibility as adults to take a continuous self-inventory. Important reminder—if you need breaks along your healing journey, that's OK. There are times when a break is needed to make room for further clarity.

### *Action Step*

Take a few minutes and write a list of the things people do that trigger you on a level that seems more intense than it may need to be. After making a list of these behaviors, take a minute and see if there is any correlation to something that you struggle with within yourself.

Here's an example: Mike has a close friend, Tom, with whom he spends a great deal of time. They share a lot of common interests and feelings on different topics. One of the things Mike struggles with most about Tom is his desire to make a plan for everything. When Tom does this, Mike has an intense reaction of anger and then feels extremely guilty for lashing out at his friend. When working with Mike, we took a look at patterns in his life and explored that as a young boy he felt his parents planned everything so stringently that there was very little room for things to develop naturally. As a result, Mike's "little rebellious boy" comes out when he feels he has no room for spontaneity. He then beats himself up for being angry because he sees no reason for it, logically. What Mike was able to learn was that he didn't feel his need for freedom as a child was honored. Then, when he feels that need being threatened as an adult, he reacts with anger—and guilt ensues because his adult self knows this is not about the current situation. We explored how his anger from not having his needs met when he was younger or feeling seen by his parents was behind this issue. Once he realized the anger was a result of his "little boy" when he was nine, he was able to take time when he felt anger and acknowledge it through soothing self-talk instead of experiencing a negative narrative.

*Notes:*

## *Connecting with Self: Feelings*

Feelings can test our ability to be patient. In our culture, we've been taught that thoughts are very powerful, driving much of our lives. But do we know how to master the mind? And how do thoughts relate to feelings? Do thoughts dictate feelings or vice versa? Navigating this can be tricky.

Many people that I've worked with spend a lot of time thinking about how they feel instead of actually feeling how they feel. This is considered a spiritual or emotional override—when we spend more time in our heads and less time in our hearts. Our "busy culture" ideal is what causes many to live in fear, anxiety, and dis-ease with self. When we are constantly striving toward our goals or spending time in distraction, we take ourselves away from self, further detaching from our truth and intuition. We are not allowing for the opportunity to tune in to what the body is saying, or how we are truly feeling.

What are our needs at any given moment? Do you know what your needs are?

We regularly hear people speak of how we need to integrate the mind, body, and spirit. The challenge for most—including myself at different times in my life—is learning how to incorporate awareness and real-life application. We all know that our bodies require fuel to move forward, yet on a regular basis we ignore what our bodies are trying to tell us. Then, we wonder why we experience disease and sickness. What would the world be like if we spent as much effort in caring for ourselves as we currently do in distraction? It is not our "fault"—it's no one's fault, per se; it's simply the nature of our culture. We are constantly moving fast from one thing to the next with an infinite number of distractions along the way—smartphones, tablets, emails, texts, and that delicious new series you're dying to binge-watch.

The key is knowing where to start.

The best place to begin is while in conversation with someone. Pay attention to your thoughts.

Are you truly listening to them or are you thinking about the to-do list that isn't getting done because you are part of this conversation? Are you out to dinner with a friend and they are speaking but you are too busy checking out the TV that's above the bar for the scores of your favorite team? These are examples of places where you can heighten your awareness as to how "in the moment" you are. It is a basic action step, only requiring you to determine what your thoughts are in that moment so that you can see what distracts you and what you need in order to change it. For some, changing this behavior means taking time to think about what you have on your to-do list before you commit to making plans.

***Use this time to write down the thoughts that run through your head, taking you out of the moments you're wanting to enjoy.***

## *Learning from Behavior*

There's another layer of complexity when it comes to "feeling our feelings," and that is about tuning in. As we learn to tune into our body, we must also tune into our behaviors, and the thoughts driving it all.

Here is an example of my work with a client, progressing from the behaviors to thought patterns to the method for growing beyond the learned modes of unconscious action—and finally to a place of empowerment.

## *Case Study: "Margaret"*

Margaret came to me, struggling with feeling she is not respected at home. We processed how she communicates with her husband and kids, which reinforces giving her power away. Some examples of language she has used that exhibit this might sound like, "Kids, it would be really nice if you could clean up your rooms today." In this example, Margaret expected her children to clean their rooms, but she is not communicating that expectation clearly. Therefore, this allowed the children to perceive this as a choice—not an expectation. We then discussed specific ways to communicate that allow her to take her power back and not be pushed aside. Regarding her children cleaning their rooms, she felt comfortable with the rephrase being, "Kids, your rooms need to be cleaned today by dinnertime. Cleaning means everything off the floor, dirty clothes in the hamper, clean clothes put away, and dust." We processed the way this statement allows her to be strong in her parenthood and explored that when we give our power away, we give people no reason to respect us, as we are showing them we don't respect ourselves. Determining the action steps you want to take for growth requires you to honestly and intentionally assess the belief systems you learned growing up that are assimilated into your behavior. In Margaret's case, she grew up with seven siblings, and when she felt disrespected, she became quieter and more distant. This reinforced a lack of respect in her relationships as she didn't use her voice and felt no one stood up for her.

It is through the discovery of these belief systems, whether rational or not, that we are able to look at how our behavior and choices perpetuate the narrative and prove the validity of the original belief system. It is also in these embedded beliefs that we may misperceive and misunderstand the intention of others in our intimate relationships. This is where projection can become prevalent. Psychological projection is misinterpreting what is "inside" as coming from the "outside." It is derived from a past wound from which we project our insecurities onto others—as our reality can be distorted by our past experiences. Once we begin to see the presuppositions in our thoughts and actions, we can start to analyze and grow beyond the preconceived assumptions. We tend to view life through the lens of our experiences and our wounds. The traumas and pain can often play a large role in how we hear, see, feel, and understand our partners and our relationships. The wounds sustained are typically a result of the belief systems we have grown up with and then played out throughout our lives. Once we are able to identify these patterns, we are able to look at the healing that needs to take place. We can also determine the boundaries we need to set in order to do this work. By connecting with self, we can tap into our "gut voice," the inner voice that knows where it wants to go, how it wants to love, and what it seeks in this world.

**Write about areas in which you would like to communicate more directly and what holds you back from doing so.**

# Chapter Three

## BOUNDARIES & INTUITION

Boundaries are exhausting as we learn them—and exhilarating when we are able to set them. Like it or not, it's the truth. Our boundaries are based on our intuition and needs. And it's not easy or simple to define them, articulate our boundaries to others, and hold the line when they are breached.

This is work.

People throw the word *boundaries* around repeatedly, and yet most people do not understand what a boundary is—or what "having boundaries" means. How can you let someone know what your boundaries are when you aren't in touch with what you need and you don't know your body's cues? Furthermore, how can you know when your intuition is telling you something isn't right if you don't have any boundaries? If we continue to relinquish our boundaries, we are left feeling empty because boundaries serve as a form of emotional protection. Without them, we are left open. Once we examine these things, we are then faced with the choice as to whether or not we honor the needs that require those boundaries. It is when we do not honor the knowledge we have obtained about ourselves that we must live with feelings of sadness, anxiety, and unnecessary discontent. The answer? We must simply learn to listen.

A patient of mine recently went away on a "guys trip." He went on a whitewater rafting trip at an eco spa within the state with friends from work—

men of varying ages and backgrounds from his office design team. In our session we explored the fact that he was preoccupied with being a part of the team on the trip, even though it was more of an impromptu weekend away as opposed to a team-building event. The entire long weekend, he was concerned about being part of everything they were scheduling, and trying desperately not to miss out on anything. He then noticed that he became irritable as he was ignoring his own need to have some alone time to decompress. The fact was that he was extremely stressed out from work that weekend. He was also dealing with some issues at home that were worrying him. What he really needed was to take advantage of the time away from his family to just "chill." Instead, he ignored his own needs and boundaries, which led him to become short-tempered and, ultimately, miserable. He had a terrible time because of it.

Part of self-care is establishing solid boundaries and looking out for the clues that define your needs. Acknowledging that he was just dog-tired—or emotionally spent and had nothing left to give—were my patient's particular signs that he needed to let go and step away from the whirlwind of activities and just "be." Awareness is the lynchpin. Once you can tune into your feelings in any given moment, you are able to set your boundaries to protect yourself. It may be that you simply need a hot shower, a walk, or a nap. It doesn't matter which form of self-care you choose; you just need to acknowledge that a "time-out" is needed, to rest and recuperate.

***Do you struggle to hold a boundary? Why?***

## *Action Step: Setting a Boundary*

Your spouse asks if you could make an impromptu dinner for his sister's birthday—with only a day's notice. You are in the middle of an important work project that will be all-consuming for the next week. In your mind you are thinking, *I asked you last week about your sister's birthday—and you just brushed it off, saying something about the fact that she had other plans.* Instead of blurting out expletives in anger, you take a pause and say, "Honey, I have so much work over the next week—I'm not going to be able to plan, shop, and cook for a birthday party. Next time you need me to help with something like this, I'll need more notice; not one day before." In this response you are showing that you respect your time just as much as you respect his. You are setting the boundary in a kind and loving way, letting him know that you are happy to help but cannot do so at the last minute due to his lack of planning. You will never regret setting healthy boundaries. As you continue to "hear" what you need, your boundaries will come to fruition. Don't be hard on yourself if it takes time. It's a practice that is never perfect—but absolutely necessary.

***What is a new boundary you can set and how will you stick to it?***

# Chapter Four

## RESENTMENT

Resentment is defined as "bitter indignation at having been treated unfairly." The difficulty most people have in grasping the concept of resentment is that it starts within us. We become resentful of others when we neglect to identify and hold our boundaries, leading to a feeling of being mistreated. Very often, resentment occurs when we ignore our gut instinct telling us that something isn't right. For some, that may manifest as a feeling of nausea, and for others it may be heart palpitations. When we are in tune enough with our bodies and listen to its signals that something isn't right—and then ignore that cue and go along with whatever feels wrong—we tend to look at the person who has asked us to comply as if it's their fault. Projection, yet again. When we disregard our own needs, the only person we have to be upset or frustrated with is us. At the end of the day, no one can "make us" do anything we don't want to do. Typically, when we engage in something we don't want to, it is rooted in fear of the perceived consequence of us not going along with it. We may feel that we are missing out; we won't be loved or won't feel like we belong. Those dreaded results are largely driven by our own narratives that stem from the belief systems we have developed and replayed throughout our lives. Yes . . . we are back to the belief systems pattern of behavior.

## *Action Step*

Write down a list of who you are mad at and why. Leave space under each person's name and the explanation of why they upset you. Underneath the names and the "whys," I want you to write down how you ignored yourself, which is what led to why you are mad at someone else.

## *Notes:*

# Chapter Five

**EMOTIONAL READINESS**

You can't make someone willing to "see" something if they are not ready. We have all had that experience. We tell a loved one something that we observe, such as a situation they are in or an emotional challenge they are experiencing, and we think they hear us. Later on, they may tell us, "My therapist said . . . and I get it." At that moment, we may be secretly trying not to harbor resentment while thinking, *What? I said that to you years ago!* The reality is that they needed it to be said at that time, by that person, and in that circumstance to be able to "hear" it. No one person has any power over you. When you are ready and able to receive information to grow on your journey, you will hear it.

For some of us, it takes getting a divorce, losing your father, and starting your own business within a nine-month period for you to truly be "woke." Yes, it wasn't until that moment that I learned to surrender to the universe because I had no idea what was going on and where I was headed. It took multiple crises to learn the true depths of myself in ways that I never thought possible. The universe is always talking to us, and yet at this pivotal moment, I realized that I had spent the better part of forty years of my life ignoring what it was saying.

How does the universe talk to us? It speaks to us in ways that it thinks we can hear. For me, this meant "listening" to certain clues, observing repetitive numbers or particular animals that showed up in my life at pivotal moments. My first experience in listening to the universe happened after my father died. I was pulled over by a police officer for speeding, not once but twice within five days. My dad was a very well-respected New York detective and I had no question in my mind that this was my dad saying, "Slow down." He knew I could "hear" this sign loud and clear. Another way in which the universe was communicating with me was when I would see feathers in the most unexpected places, where it made no sense to see one. Feathers are a classic sign from the universe that your angels (in this case, my father) are with you, and the particular color of the feather carries a spiritual meaning.

Your ability to listen to the universe, God, or whatever higher power you may believe in requires you to have faith in something outside of yourself. I believe in the energy of the universe and our ability to tap into that if we so wish. In the beginning of my spiritual journey, some may have thought I was out of my mind. I was continuously reading up on the spiritual meaning of signs I saw, and then trying to decipher what the universe was saying. For a little while at the beginning of this path, I would drive myself nuts by attempting to make sense of things through my head—and not my heart. It was at this point that I had to refocus my energy on what I was feeling. I had to learn what felt good and what felt bad so I could listen to my intuition through these feelings. When I was able to truly feel in my body and listen, I was able to find my flow with the universe and the doors of opportunity opened wide.

One of my favorite lines in a movie is, "When you ask God for patience, he presents you with opportunities to be patient." This is extremely impactful. Often, people ask God or the universe to give them something—but that's not how it works.

The universe and God simply provide you with the opportunities to utilize the skills you have gained over time; they don't "do" anything for you. As previously stated, whenever we start to engage in change, the universe will tempt us with our past, as well as our old behaviors, to see how truly committed we are to our new path. That's where the golden nuggets of opportunity are found.

It is always up to us as to whether we make a healthy choice or take the opportunity in front of us. It is our responsibility to choose—and ours alone.

## *Action Step*

Patience, patience, and more patience. It can be daunting to see a block that someone else can't see—and they keep running into it. Remember, there is absolutely nothing you can do to make them see it. This is where your action step is pure love and patience. It is not your job to make them see it; it is not their active choice not to see it either. They are struggling and this is something that sits in a place they are not able to access, currently. It is their blind spot. We need to love them, give them space, and try our best not to beat the dead horse while doing it.

# *What gets in the way of your ability to be patient when someone is struggling?*

## Chapter Six

## **THE GREAT SHUTDOWN**

Speaking of patience... Have you ever been with a friend or partner, having a potentially emotional conversation, and then boom! You lost them. They are staring back at you with a blank expression on their face—a "deer in the headlights" look would be an accurate description. This is what I like to call "the great shutdown." It can be very difficult to navigate, particularly when it is a subconscious behavior for the person who has just shut down. When I say shut down, I am referring to someone who becomes overwhelmed with emotion or is triggered by something in the conversation and they emotionally "leave." This can show up as someone looking or acting lost, staring blankly into space, and being nonresponsive or disconnected from the discussion. What I want you to know is that it's not you. I repeat, it's not you. The great shutdown is a person's way of saying, "This is too much," or "I can't handle what I am feeling right now." It is extremely important for you to know this and truly embrace that it has nothing to do with you personally.

I have been the one who's shut down and I have experienced others shutting down. There are definitely times where it's difficult not to take it personally. When someone shuts down it can be extremely confusing. We are left standing there, saying to ourselves, *What just happened? I don't get it.* The best thing we can do for the one who shut down is to revisit what happened at a later date (ideally within a few days so the details are still fresh) and process it, together.

Ask them if there is anything you can do in the future, when you see them shutting down, to help ground them. Grounding techniques are things that bring someone back to the present moment. For me, when I'm upset or in an emotional discussion, having my husband just reach out and grab my hand, without a word, helps bring me back to center so I can move forward in a healthy way.

When we allow ourselves to shut down repeatedly—and some people don't even realize they are doing it—our emotions can get stuck in our bodies. This can be likened to shutting off our "emotional faucet." As we grow on our journey, we realize that if we allow our emotional faucet to get backed up, we run the great risk of bursting a metaphorical pipe. I always discuss the importance of not turning off our emotional faucet after sessions with my clients. It's essential to allow feelings to remain flowing while knowing you can control the flow. If you do not take the opportunity to do this, emotions will build and the faucet may "flood" at another time, making it difficult to parse out the difference between old emotions and current feelings.

***Write a list of the things that make you "shut down." If you aren't aware, ask someone you love and trust what those things may be and take some time to explore why they make you feel the need to shut down.***

# Chapter Seven

## GHOSTING... WHO DOES THAT?

What is a greater shutdown than ghosting? The issue of ghosting has become more prevalent in our society as technology grows. Technology has also allowed us to avoid using our communication tools to manage "the great shutdown" in a healthy way. At what point did not responding to someone become acceptable? It started in the dating scene after apps were created, and it has gained great momentum since then. I see it infecting younger generations as they "leave someone on read," which means someone has read what had been written by the sender—but they chose not to respond. The effects of ghosting leave people in a heightened state of anxiety and bewilderment. I can tell you that I have had countless sessions with clients about how they were ghosted. They don't understand what they did or why this person has not responded and it leaves a figurative open wound with no resolution. People appear to ghost others for a multitude of reasons. They didn't like what was said; they were triggered; they had some form of an emotional reaction and instead of learning a healthy way to address challenges in their relationships, they simply choose to avoid and ignore the other person. This method of coping is ineffective and fuels the belief "If I don't want to deal with it, I don't have to." As a result, we are hurting others by causing unnecessary anxiety and overthinking only because we have not learned healthy conflict resolution and communication skills. If there is one potential silver lining to being ghosted, it is that it creates a space for us to learn how to manage our thoughts and find closure without someone giving us the opportunity. Oftentimes, when we do not have the ability to say the things that we wanted to say, or finish a discussion, we feel as though our thoughts and feelings don't matter. We feel unheard—and that feels awful.

## *Action Step*

If you have been ghosted, as most of us have at some point, then here is a place to start in finding closure. Write your "ghoster" a letter. Don't worry about proper English, grammar, or placement of your periods—just write. During this process, allow yourself to feel the emotions, let the tears flow, and don't stop until you feel all that needs to be said is on paper. Take the letter and put it aside in a safe place for a few days or so. Revisit the letter and read it aloud to yourself. Once again, feel what comes up. After this step you can choose to send your letter—or burn it and "say goodbye." The art of writing the letter is not necessarily to give it to your ghoster; it is to allow yourself the closure you need in order to move on. Believe me, it works if you allow it to.

***Notes:***

## Chapter Eight

**PEOPLE PLEASING**

We have to be honest with ourselves so that we can be honest about ourselves with others. When someone is engaging in "people pleasing" behavior, it's a defense mechanism that has been developed over time to protect them from pain or from unpleasant feelings. The challenge with this coping skill is that for the "people pleaser" their best intentions are only to make their partner or loved one happy. Yet, as a result, this creates an illusion for their loved one, as they truly believe that the people pleaser genuinely believes or feels the way they say they do. When, in reality, there are times that they don't actually believe what they are saying or doing at all, and it is purely a function to minimize or eliminate discomfort. In a relationship dynamic, this creates a foundation based on unintentional deception. The "people pleaser" is not being authentic and, as a result, their partner or loved one is in a relationship with someone that is not the person they believe them to be. This can be extremely confusing.

Let me give you an example: A husband comes home from work, exhausted and irritable. His wife greets him kindly and proceeds to ask him how his day was, as he snaps at her and responds in a way that doesn't feel good. It honestly pisses her off. Later, her husband comes to her and says, "Honey, I'm sorry I was snappy before." And she replies with, "Don't worry about it; it was fine." Who is engaging in people pleasing? His wife is.

I'm not implying there needs to be a fight and her response to his apology should have been, "Yeah, you were really nasty," but what I am saying is that when he apologized, it was an opportunity for her to say "thank you for the apology because that really didn't feel good." This response gives her the chance to be open and honest about her feelings, with love and compassion. However, it also allows her to be authentic as to how it made her feel. I have seen this behavior in many marriages, and I have seen many marriages end in divorce because the person who has been engaging in people pleasing as a coping skill gets to a point where they are having trouble living in their own skin. Anger and resentment ensue until it becomes intolerable. As a result of this emotional buildup, they ultimately get to a place of "that's it, I'm done." When we people please, we ignore our needs. Inevitably, we get to a breaking point. It is saddening to see marriages break up as a result of this behavior because more often than not it is unintentional and a learned behavior.

So how do you *unlearn* this behavior?

## *Action Step*

If you find yourself in this situation with someone in your life whom you love a great deal and you feel they are engaging in people pleasing, you can start by asking them either of the following questions:

1. "Is this how you truly feel or do you need this discussion to pause for a little bit to collect your thoughts?"

2. "What do you want, or need, right now?"

Monitor your reaction to these conversations to see what role you may be playing in the behavior. For example, are you a screamer? If so, over time you may see that the more you scream the more your partner engages in people pleasing. If you are the person who engages in people pleasing, which we all do at times and in different circumstances, it is important for you to PAUSE. Meaning, if you are in a discussion and it is not feeling good (your stomach is turning; you feel like you have to go to the bathroom; you are getting physically hot), your body is telling you something is not right and that's your cue to say, "I need some time to think about this and I will come back to you when I'm able to articulate my thoughts."

This is just a template. I encourage you to use your own words, but you can view this as a guide. How we say things can truly make or break a situation, so taking a pause is crucial.

***When do you engage in people pleasing and why?***

# Chapter Nine

**INTENTION**

Intention is the difference in the direction we take in our relationships and in the health of our choices. We are consistently asked to look at what our intentions are, in what we say, what we do, and how we treat others. When your intention is pure, there should be no fault in what you are doing. It's when intention is impure and manipulative that questions come into play about a simple situation. You are out with friends for the evening. You are married, and you are flirting with multiple people at the bar. Do you think to yourself, *If my partner were to do this to me, I would be extremely upset*? And yet you continue to engage in the behavior. This is a point where you should ask yourself, *What is my intention? What am I needing while engaging in this interaction?*

Another example: You are speaking with a friend, exploring how you felt about the situation that happened between the two of you. During this discussion, you speak to your friend in a passive-aggressive way. What was your intention in being passive-aggressive? Was it truly to find resolution to the situation? Or were you trying to hurt them so that you're not the only one who is hurt? These are the things that are important to consider in our daily choices—and in all the words that we say.

It's also important to understand that when your intention to love and understand fades—are you able to show up as your best self?

## *Action Step*

Think about your most recent disagreement with a loved one. Write down all the different ways in which you reacted and how you spoke to them. After you complete your list, look back at each action or set of words, and beside each one, write what your intention was in that moment. Do this while it is fresh in your mind. After reviewing your list and your intentions, check to see if there is congruence between your behavior and your intentions. If they are not akin to one another, this is where the next step of your journey begins.

### *Notes:*

# Chapter Ten

## COMMUNICATION 101

I can't tell you how many times I've been in session with clients when they are relaying a discussion they had and I asked them, "Did you say that to your partner?" And the response is often, "Well . . . I think I did . . ." When we are processing an exchange in session, it gives us the ability to look at our words and how we communicate our intentions, thoughts, and feelings.

What I have realized in my work—and in my personal life—is that we aren't always communicating as clearly as we think we are. Within the dynamics of our relationships, we can say one thing and often mean another—but become confused as to why the person doesn't understand what we're saying. That's because we're likely not communicating in a clear and effective manner. So how do we fix this? By asking people what they are hearing after we have said something.

It is in these moments after we say something important that we can ask, "What did you just hear?" That way, we can determine if our message was effectively communicated or not. If it was not, it is our job to look at how we can say it differently, and with more clarity.

### *What You're Hearing Is Probably Not the Issue . . .*

The way in which we communicate, and our ability to truly hear what is being said, shapes how we show up in our relationships on differing levels. I do a lot of work with couples. One of the main themes that we deal with is that a topic of discussion is very rarely what is at the core of the challenge they face.

As human beings, we spend a lot of time talking about a particular situation and specific actions that someone engaged in that pissed us off—and yet when we sift through the surface details, the core is underlying and not being spoken of because it requires vulnerability. That's the scary part.

I had a couple in my office the other day and they were arguing about how each of them responded to an extremely stressful situation they had encountered. They were in the midst of the flu running rampant through their home and they were functioning in survival mode. Here is a taste of their discussion in my office that day:

Wife: "You know, I was really ill and you just ignored how sick I was!"

Husband: "No I didn't. I was doing my best to work and take care of the kids—who were also sick. And you can be dramatic when you don't feel well."

Wife: "What?!?! Yes, maybe I can be dramatic on occasion but this time I was really sick and you didn't show any acknowledgment of that—until I went to the hospital to get hydrated."

Husband: "Honey, you're always in the bathroom. How am I supposed to know when it's different? You didn't say anything."

I sat back and allowed the discussion to play out for a little while. It is during the "play-out" that I am able to see the theme and then strategically jump in. At the core of their exchange is the wife wanting to be nurtured, seen, and cared for when she doesn't feel well. When we explored this further, what evolved was how she has been very guarded with her husband. As a result, she doesn't speak up to be nurtured and therefore her husband doesn't know that this is her need—let alone how to meet it.

Her "guardedness" stems from patterns of behavior she learned growing up. But what once kept her safe in the past is now getting in her way in the present. When I jumped in and asked her, "Did you tell your husband what you needed from him?" she replied, "No." After addressing the fact that if we don't communicate our needs we can't expect someone to meet them, we then explored what nurturing looks like to her.

We also discussed concrete behaviors her husband could engage in that would let her know he hears her and is nurturing her.

We all have one particular topic in our relationship that rears its ugly head, over and over again, and yet we still can't seem to find a resolution. The reality is, what you're discussing is not the real issue, which is why you keep having the same conversation multiple times. Seeing the core of the discussion requires both parties to be able to truly listen without ego, old wounds, defense mechanisms, and all of the other baggage that goes along with it. This may sound like I'm saying, "Oh yeah, after all these years of fighting over the same issue I will just let everything go and it will be fine." I know that's not reality.

What I am saying is that it requires commitment to practice together.

## *Action Step*

Disclaimer: Try this only if you feel as though you are in a relationship that is emotionally safe. To me, emotionally safe refers to feeling that your vulnerability will be met with love and compassion. The best place to start this practice is by sitting down with your partner facing each other and holding hands. Do this when you are both in a "good place" emotionally. There should not have been an argument within the last twenty-four to forty-eight hours that will creep into this practice. Pick a benign topic such as the shirt you or your partner is wearing, which you don't like (just an example so you get the idea). Practice by having one of you say to the other how you feel about the shirt and the person receiving the message is to simply listen while facing their partner. Remain holding hands for as long as you can tolerate.

Then take some time away from the discussion and within twenty-four hours come back together and try this again.

This time, the partner who listened gets to speak their truth about how it felt to hear what was said about their shirt—and their partner will do the listening. Very often when we hear something that we perceive as hurtful, our instinct is to emotionally run away, shut down, or deflect. Try this once a week, and each week use a topic that may be a little more challenging emotionally.

Whenever we struggle to hear someone we love express how they feel, it is typically because some part of us was triggered and we need to understand what the trigger was that evoked the reaction. This requires time, space, and our ability to be honest with ourselves as to the source of our reactions and accompanying emotions.

***What topics in your relationship are difficult for you to communicate clearly? What is the core need that you are trying to have met?***

# Chapter Eleven

## CONGRUENCE WITH SELF AND THE WORLD AROUND US

A lack of congruence between what we say and how we behave has everything to do with feeling safe to let down our "armor." This helps us create a space that is emotionally safe. Some of the most defensive and guarded people (my prior self included) are the most kind and loving souls that have learned to protect themselves by appearing "tough" and unaffected by the behavior of others.

In working with clients for over twenty years, I have seen some of the most amazing people and transformations take place. These transformations can only occur when someone ultimately feels safe enough to let down their "armor" so they may be truly seen.

This shows up in many of my clients, but one specifically comes to mind. I had seen a young man for a few years on and off when he felt he needed some time for reflection, and there was a specific area in which he wanted to grow. In earlier sessions we would explore what he thought his "armor" might be. Through our sessions, he realized that he felt as though it was his attitude; that nothing anyone says hurts him.

As we explored this, he was able to connect how this defense mechanism came about as he was growing up. He realized that when he was younger, if he showed his family that he was "sensitive" it would be used against him in an argument, and he would be made fun of for being a "girl" and showing emotion.

As a result of this dynamic, he learned how to act as if nothing bothered him and would provide the same reaction in all situations, which was no longer serving him and causing issues in his marriage.

One of my favorite quotes from Brené Brown applies perfectly here:

"It is a painful irony that the very things that may have kept us safe growing up ultimately get in the way of our becoming the parents, partners, and/or people that we want to be."

In session we realized that his defense mechanism of acting like nothing affects him was dramatically hurting his marriage. His wife was crying out for him to show her some emotion—particularly when it came to how he feels about her. As a result, she engaged in pushing his emotional buttons that brought him to anger, just so she could see that he cared. Unfortunately, they began engaging in an unhealthy dynamic wherein she pushed him to a point of anger just so she could get a reaction. It happened more frequently over time, minimizing space for a healthy exchange to occur.

We explored little ways that he could step outside of his comfort zone to show an emotion with his wife that still allows him to feel safe.

Some of the ideas we explored consisted of saying "I love you," telling his wife she looked beautiful when he felt it, and holding her hand when he felt close to her—even if it's only for a few seconds. Before we started this journey, we asked his wife to come in for a joint session. We needed to talk with her about what he wanted to try so she could understand and notice when he was making efforts. That way, she could also connect with him in those moments. The joint session allowed him to ask his wife for her support with his growth process—even though it may be uncomfortable at times. It also provided the space for him to help his wife understand why he appears as if he is emotionally distant—and she was able to see that it was not about her.

Watching her come to understand this information was truly transformative; I saw the guard around her heart slowly begin to disappear right before my eyes.

## Action Step

If you are looking for a wonderful resource, please read *The Knight in Rusty Armor*. This book is a tool that I encourage most clients to read as we begin a journey of transformation. Reading this book was the beginning of my journey of determining and understanding what my armor was—and to ultimately release it. It has also allowed me to help others do the same.

If you see a recurring argument happen in your life, it may be time to explore your "armor." When reading the book, take note of the things that resonate with you. It is a metaphorical journey and is a wonderful way to help you tune into your intuition. All that means is—you need to write down the thoughts that pop into your head while reading as they are coming from your intuition.

These thoughts are attempting to lead you to your answers.

When you are finished with the book, please take time for reflection and look through your notes for a theme that reoccurs.

***What is your armor and why do you use it?***

# Chapter Twelve

## COMPASSION FOR HEALTHY RELATIONSHIPS

Healing often requires us to care for our inner child, as opposed to seeking change externally. When we learn how to hear and soothe our injured little child inside of us, we are able to create emotional safety—not only for ourselves but also for others in our intimate lives. How can we effectively accept and love all parts of our loved ones if we are not able to love all parts of ourself? Full disclosure: we can't.

Don't get me wrong—acceptance is no easy feat, but we can start by hearing what our inner child is telling us. Pay attention when you have reactions that make you think, *Where did that come from?* Odds are, it came from your inner child who is asking to be seen and nurtured by your adult self.

I work with many relationships where one individual in the partnership has difficulty being kind to themselves and, as a result, this manifests in an inability to be kind to their partner. This is a major issue. If someone was raised with a "you need to buck up and deal with it" belief system, it reinforces a notion that they are not allowed to have feelings—and they need to ignore their instincts. It follows, then, that this individual may struggle with empathy or compassion, particularly when their partner is anxious about something. This stoic belief system makes it nearly impossible to connect and hold space for someone when it seems like feelings shouldn't matter. The overriding sense of things for this person is that they should just put their head down and "take care of business."

## *Action Step: Compassion in a Relationship*

Imagine that you come home from work and your partner begins venting to you about how difficult their day was—and they just need a break. You stand at the door thinking, *What the hell—I just walked through the door and you hit me with this? My day was no walk in the park!* However, you choose to keep those thoughts to yourself and practice pure empathy.

I would ask you to consider engaging in a behavior with your partner that you sense would be what feels best to them by asking, "What do you need?" By asking your partner what they need, you are taking a step back and not allowing their emotions to escalate and have a strong effect on you. You are also helping your loved one to tune in with themselves and get to their gut instinct. You are allowing them to be able to identify their need and then verbalize it. This way, you are taking the opportunity to show your partner you hear them by honoring the need they stated. It may mean taking over a household chore, cuddling with them, or making dinner—so it's one less thing they need to worry about. By engaging in these activities you will make a world of difference in the connection you have with your loved one. This will also model the behavior that you wish to be reciprocated when the tables are turned. Modeling the behavior we desire in our lives is key to getting—and keeping—the kind of relationships we want.

Once we master these skills, it is important to see how they are showing us a piece of our inner child that needs to be healed. The example of this lies in the partner's internal dialogue of "my day was no walk in the park!" By taking time to examine and heal this part of ourselves, it will decrease reactions in the future. It can feel difficult at first, but you will be glad you reached within and extended safety and support for yourself, as well as your partner.

**Write about the ways you struggle to show yourself compassion. Are these the same areas in which you struggle to show others compassion?**

# Chapter Thirteen

## RELATIONSHIP BELIEF SYSTEMS

We all hear people—particularly women—talk about "daddy issues." "Oh yeah, you have daddy issues." Or, "Don't marry him; he has mommy issues." I find it so interesting that we neglect to acknowledge the effect that our relationship with our same-sex parent can have on us. The relationship with our same-sex parent largely dictates how we show up in the world as a male or female. We watch our mothers interact with our fathers and learn a great deal about what a woman or man "should be"—in a marriage or relationship. These are all wonderful gifts, and yet, as we mature, if we aren't self-aware, we may take on some of our parents' beliefs and habits without even knowing it. At the end of the day, a daughter's relationship with her mother is extremely complex. In working with women of varying ages, they often realize they have shown up in their intimate relationships similarly to their mother—without being aware of it—and vice versa for men.

When I work with both men and women, exploring behavior and beliefs systems, I find that the majority of patterns develop when we are young, watching our parents interact within the family system. This is a perfect example of practice what you preach. As children, we essentially study our parents' every move and are eager to learn. When we do not take time to reflect on why we are making the choices we make or engaging in the behaviors we do, we are allowing unhealthy generational habits to persist.

I saw this in an intense way when I was working with my client Kathy. Kathy was in her mid-fifties and had just lost her mom to cancer. During our time together we explored that when she was growing up, she would watch her mother cater to her father's every need. Kathy grew up in a traditional home where her mother's job was to raise the children and keep a clean house while her father worked to support the family financially. As we explored her upbringing, she would drift off into memories of watching her mother iron her father's clothes, packing his lunch for work, and making sure the house was quiet when he got home because he had worked a long day. As we looked more closely at how this had impacted Kathy's life, she was able to realize that she internalized her mother's behavior as a wife. The belief was that women existed only to take care of their men and children—and that was their sole purpose in life. This belief system caused Kathy difficulty when she was married when she realized that she needed to work outside the home to earn a salary so they could survive. During this time, she became more and more resentful because she believed that her husband should earn enough so she wouldn't have to work, and unfortunately that wasn't the case. She realized that her belief system was based on what she observed growing up, and in her mind, working equated to her feeling that she wasn't a good mother.

## *Action Step*

Write a list of the roles that your same-sex parent engaged in while you were growing up. After you complete this list, write a separate list as to the roles you have taken on in your intimate relationship. Look at these lists in order to compare and contrast so you have the awareness to decide if you are engaging in a role purely due to the way you were raised or if it's a role to which you genuinely consented. If your response when looking at these lists is, "This is not what I signed up for," then it's the perfect opportunity to ask your partner to make the same lists. Then, you both need to come together to discern what roles work best for you as individuals, and then as a couple.

## Notes:

# Chapter Fourteen

## OUR TRIGGERS; OUR CHANGES

If we want a relationship to change, then we need to show up differently. It isn't until we change that we can then truly assess whether the relationship still feels right—or if it's a relationship that we need to let go of. What do I mean by "show up differently"? It's about our reactions and how we change them. The old saying "it takes two to tango" is entirely valid in this scenario.

We must take a good look at the metaphorical dance we do with the people in our lives. For example, when I was growing up, my dad was a true ballbuster—and that's what we all loved about him—unless it was directed at us kids, of course. When it was directed at me, I took the bait every time and twice on Sunday, and then wondered why he kept doing it. Well, he kept doing it because it filled his need of getting me fired up. And my intense reaction (though it got me in trouble many times) provided the reinforcement required to encourage the unrelenting ball-busting. Changing our reaction can be quite tricky, of course. Particularly if we are out of tune with what our triggers might be.

Yes, I said *trigger* . . .

Triggers are something you need to lean into—and allow—not hide behind. I am an intense person on a good day, so when I experience an emotion, it is clear to those around me what it is. No one would accuse me of being shy; it's not my forte. Now, as charming as this quality can be, it has definitely gotten me into trouble. As a result, I have had to train myself to use the pause. I learned to do this by first examining why I was so triggered by what was said or done. I take time at some point during the day of the occurrence to reflect on what happened and why I had such an intense reaction. I then take time to process this with someone I trust, typically the person with whom I reacted to, and then explore how it played out and what my role was in the situation. After the processing discussion, I continue to look further—and seek support from outsiders if necessary—as to what I need to nurture in myself in order to lessen my reaction in the future.

For example, my son woke up one day before band practice. He was exhausted that morning and was trying to get out of going.

"I don't want to do band anymore; it's boring and I'm over it!"

The initial reaction in my mind was, *Oh, hell no! You've committed so you will see this through!* But thankfully, that was not what came out of my mouth. Instead, I was curious and asked, "Why?

Where is this coming from?" As parents (myself included at times), our initial reaction can often be the need to teach our children a lesson. Because everything these days is a "teachable moment," isn't it? But some of the best teachable moments are when we keep our mouths shut and allow our curiosity to take over. So that's what I did.

After listening for some time, and processing alone later that day, I was able to hear what he truly needed and see that my trigger and subsequent reaction was based on the value I uphold about being a person of integrity and seeing commitments through. The importance of this example is that I chose to listen instead of allowing my trigger to take over, which gave me the opportunity to connect with my son instead of creating a disconnect. That way, I wasn't functioning out of a trigger—but out of curiosity. By allowing him time to express his feelings without being shut down, he eventually came to the conclusion on his own—that he ultimately wanted to fulfill his commitment. He just needed to be heard.

# Write a list of values you hold that make it hard for you to listen to others and why.

Chapter Fourteen

## *Yes, You Can Be Seen and Heard*

We talk about connection a lot these days, and yet we are missing opportunities for connection all the time. We miss these opportunities when we are too busy thinking about something else while our loved one or friend is talking to us. When we are watching a video on YouTube and our loved one asks a question and we don't pause it to truly hear what's being asked. When we are scrolling on Facebook and our mother calls to catch up and we continue to scroll. These are concrete examples of missed opportunities for connection. Unfortunately, the message we are sending to our loved one is, "You're not important enough for me to stop what I'm doing." Yes, that's how it feels; and that feels awful.

I worked with an extremely insightful young man for quite some time who would continually impress me with wisdom beyond his years. During one of our sessions, we explored that while he was away at college, he would find reasons to call home to talk to his father because he missed him. But he didn't actually communicate that he missed him, nor did his father see the attempt being made at connection. We discussed how his relationship with his father was not an emotional one, and when he tried to show emotion, his dad would encourage his son to talk to his mother—and get off the phone quickly. We looked at the fact that, as a result, he tried to find things that interested his father in order to connect with him. When taking this into a deeper layer, he had an epiphany that when looking at his peer relationships, he would subconsciously look for ways to connect with friends around their interests—ultimately losing sight of his own. In his male relationships, it reinforced a feeling that people would only like him if he showed interest in what they want or enjoy. However, if he showed emotion with males, they would have difficulty tolerating that emotion. He internalized this as something "wrong" with him, which is not the case. This belief system has been reinforced in his interactions. When he would take the risk of expressing any form of emotion, he could feel his peers' discomfort. As a result, they would emotionally distance from him, and he was left feeling even more alone. The ability for him to realize this pattern of behavior was extremely freeing for him. We explored that if he focused his energy on people who can't handle emotion, and internalize it as something that he had done wrong, he would continue the same pattern. Now that he is empowered by this knowledge, he can choose whom he engages with more strategically so that the belief system shifts. He can choose to surround himself with people who are able to see his attempts at connection and who respond in a way that feels good.

We can't change people, but we can show up differently, and ultimately, the dynamic will change.

### *Action Step*

Take a look at your social circle and the people with whom you choose to spend your time. Pick your top five closest friends and make a list of how each of them makes you feel when you are together. If the majority of the feelings you have when you are with them are ones that steal from your emotional bucket then it may be time to reevaluate the level of closeness you share.

Keep in mind that friendships, like everything else, are on a continuum. I'm not saying drop all your friends and find new ones. I am saying it might be time to feel and discern how they support you or bring you down, and then make your choices accordingly.

***Notes:***

# Chapter Fifteen

## GROUNDING IN LIFE TRANSITIONS

Finding a feeling of safety during life transitions can be extremely challenging, particularly when you're facing changes that aren't going as planned. Or perhaps your anxiety is in high gear because you have no idea what will happen on the other side. We have all experienced this at some point in our lives, whether it is accepting a new job, learning a new sport or activity, getting into a new relationship, entering or leaving a pandemic ... the list goes on. When we are about to begin a transition or find ourselves in the middle of a major shift, emotions run high. The perfect storm for overthinking. As human beings, when we become anxious, fearful, or uncomfortable with the unknown, we have a tendency to strive for determining what will happen, wondering how this will turn out or how it will end.

As a result of our discomfort, we try to find ways in which we feel in control of our lives. For some, that might be keeping their house perfectly clean at all times, and for others that means finding distractions from their emotions, such as working more than usual. It is not uncommon when we feel we aren't grounded to reach for ways to calm the discomfort and try to create a sense of control. As children, we learn how to regulate our emotions through external means, such as our parents, which we then incorporate as our own internal mode. As adults we can see this play out similarly. In an ideal world, we all know on an intellectual level that when we are at peace with ourselves nothing should be able to shake that peace. That sounds fabulous—and an achievement we would all like to feel. In the meantime, it is important to look at how we can help ourselves when we don't feel grounded in order to build and solidify that inner peace we strive for.

During the pandemic, I worked with a young lady who was struggling with anxiety regarding her performance at work. She had a persistent feeling that she was failing. We explored how working remotely did not provide her with the regular feedback from her boss that helped her to build confidence in what she was doing. When she received this feedback in the past, through conversations, facial expressions, a smile, and other nonverbal cues, it helped center her. Now that she was working remotely in her home, isolated from all of her coworkers and her boss, she felt lost. We discussed what she needed in order to feel grounded and as if she were continuing to achieve her career goals. What we came up with was to have a discussion with her boss about her need to have consistent check-ins via Zoom to discuss projects they were working on, expectations of her boss, and if she is meeting the needs of the company.

We took some time to role-play this discussion to help her tune in to her needs and feel grounded as well as to express her needs in an appropriate way. During our next session, she was feeling a great deal better as she was able to have the conversation we practiced, and felt as though it was well received.

One of the biggest points of focus during a time of transition is determining what we have the ability to influence and what we cannot. A time of transition is an ideal opportunity to effect change, and subsequently, reveal our ability to shape the outcome. One of my favorite quotes is, "People often fear change because they focus on what they have to lose instead of what they have to gain." Truth. If what we focus on grows, then we know that we need to spend our time focusing on gratitude for what brings us joy, for the fact that we wake up each morning, and that we have what we need to survive. When we are struggling, we have to get back to the "gratitude basics," such as gratitude for having food, for instance, and build from there. There is a great deal of validity in starting your day with bringing to mind one to three things that you are grateful for, and ending your day in the same way.

## *Action Step*

If you find yourself in the midst of a transition, think about what makes you feel centered, safe, and what creates a sense of calm. For some people it's cuddling with their partner. For others, it can be alone time reading a favorite book. Or it may be engaging in a conversation or activity that feels familiar. As simple as it may seem, those are your answers—doing more of what makes you feel safe and whole. As you continue to do those things, take time to think about what you want on the other side of this transition.

When you are clear about what you want, even if it's just one thing you want to achieve, then think about how you will realize it. It may be helpful to complete a vision board. The beauty of a vision board is you can cut out words and pictures from magazines, and write your own inspirational phrases on the board as well. It's the perfect opportunity to create a visual representation, reminding you of where you are headed so you don't lose sight of your aspirations.

***Write a list below of what makes you feel safe and grounded.***

# Chapter Sixteen

## HEALING THROUGH DEATH

The death of my father has been, by far, one of the most difficult things I have had to deal with in my life. At the ripe young age of thirty-nine, I lost my father to cancer. My father, a New York detective through and through, could determine your character within seconds of meeting you. And he had a look that would melt the heart of the most hardened criminal.

He loved his family more than anything in the world. Without question, I was "daddy's little girl," and that was a huge part of my identity growing up as the middle child with two brothers. Most would say that my father and I were a lot alike—and when I was in my dreaded teenage years, we would butt heads as a result. One of the many things I didn't realize when I was younger— but was able to see as I grew older—was that my father had one of the best gut instincts of anyone I knew. For all of us children, this had its pros and cons, especially when we were trying to get away with something. Due to his amazing gift, my father was able to see things that other people couldn't and he was able to solve crimes that were unsolvable for years. I believe it was because he saw people at their core. I was one of those people. My father understood me in a way that even I wasn't able to understand, until I was much older and started a family of my own.

Now you may be wondering why I am relating these details. I am sharing them to provide context to what follows . . .

The death of a loved one sucks, no matter what way you slice the pie. Each death we endure impacts us differently and there is no way to compare. Though well meaning in spirit, you cannot say to someone who has lost a loved one, "I understand." Because you know what? You don't. Each death we experience affects us differently—depending on the relationship we had with the deceased, how they passed, and where we are in life. It is also influenced by what age we are when they pass, what coping skills we use to get through their death, what support systems we have in place, and what we choose to do with the grieving process. Losing a parent at thirty-nine is different than losing a parent at eighteen—there is no comparison.

Watching my father suffer was awful. I wouldn't wish that experience on anyone, and yet the beauty of this time was that I got to see different parts of my father that he wouldn't otherwise show me—or anyone else, besides my mother. I took this time as an opportunity to have some difficult discussions with my father (as much as he probably wished I didn't) and to heal. It was in these times that I was able to see the man I knew as my father was inside—but didn't always get to see—due to the stress of his job.

Fast-forward to his last day with us here on earth. My dad was brought home from the hospital the day before, on hospice, and we were all gathered at my parents' house, knowing that time was precious and at any moment he would be gone. The afternoon had fast approached, and I needed to go get my son from school. However, I didn't want to leave my father for fear he would pass while I was gone. One of my best friends from college was with me and she pulled me aside and said, "Jess, you need to say to him whatever you feel is important to say now, just in case." So, I took a deep breath and went into the room where he was lying peacefully and took her advice. As I held his hand and brushed his hair across his forehead, I let him know how much I loved him. I talked to him about how I needed to leave and go get my son, but I didn't want to leave him. I also let him know I knew he was tired of fighting this.

At this point in time, he was slipping away rapidly and I squeezed him tightly and said, "Dad, you don't have to fight anymore; we will take care of Mom and she will be OK. We will all get through this together." It was seconds after I uttered these words that his breathing changed.

Within a very short period of time, he was gone. The minute I realized he had died, as I stood there with my mom and my brothers, I thought to myself, *What did I just do?*

In that moment, I realized that my dad needed me to say those words so he could pass with peace, and knowing that it would be OK for him to let go. I also realized that he needed to hear it from me. At the same moment, I was heartbroken with the realization that he was never coming back in physical form. The gift of giving my father permission to let go is a gift that I will cherish forever.

The irony is that as children we spend the better part of our early years seeking permission from our parents to be who we are meant to be.

Yet, in the end stages of life, we are still seeking permission, just in a different form.

Losing a parent changes you. For me, losing my father has brought me to new depths of my spirituality and my ability to trust in my intuition and the universe. After my father died, and I'd see feathers in the oddest places, showing up exactly when I needed them to, I realized that this was his way of talking to me and letting me know he is with me. That was the beginning of my spiritual deep dive. To be honest, I feel closer to my father now than I ever did when he was alive. For that I am truly grateful. I feel him with me and hear his voice at the most perfect moments. He has shared with me his gift of intuition and supported me on my path to study Reiki. He has shown me that even though people are no longer in their physical form, their souls remain. We just have to be willing to see, feel, and hear them. It is through this experience that I am better able to help people heal from loss, through connecting with their loved ones who have passed. What I mean by this is that one of my gifts as a Reiki practitioner is the ability to access people's loved ones who have passed and share messages with the living in order for healing to continue. It is a gift that I never could have imagined would be one I attained, but it's real and feels amazing.

Our healing doesn't need to end just because someone has physically left.

### *Action Step*

Don't wait to tell someone how you feel about them; tell them now. Show your loved ones your truth, your heart, and show them your soul. The healing can begin whenever we are ready to take a step, so start yours now.

***Write down what stops you from expressing your true love to those in your life.***

_____

_____

_____

# Chapter Seventeen

## **LOSS IS LOSS IN A DIVORCE**

Whether you are the one who chooses to get divorced or you are the one informed that your partner wants a divorce, both parties experience a sense of loss. So why do we feel the need to compare stories and determine which party hurts more, depending on whether they wanted the divorce or not? We don't engage in these discussions when someone we love dies, so why do we do it when it comes to divorce?

Regardless of your stance, there is still a grieving process that takes place. Grieving looks different for everyone, and as we know, people vacillate through the stages differently. What I have learned is that there is far less compassion in this world for the people who chose to leave the marriage. Why is that? People don't get married thinking, *Yeah, I plan to divorce them someday.*

No, of course not.

The grieving that takes place for both parties is surrounded by the loss of the life they thought they were going to have—but no longer do. Both parties are devastated by the sadness of their family breaking up and how it will affect their children. They feel confused and wonder what they did wrong, and simultaneously feel the searing pain of hurting someone they still care for, deeply. We all hide from these emotions in different ways, and in divorce it's typically hidden behind anger. It's far easier and more "tolerable" for people to support someone when they are angry as opposed to when someone is grieving.

Divorce is the death of what once was—and will no longer be. As a culture, we need to be better about honoring the intense grieving that takes place when people divorce. We also need to understand how and why it shows up through anger more often than any other emotion.

***Please explore how loss is challenging for you.***

## Chapter Eighteen

## **PARENTAL CONTROLS**

One of the most challenging things parents face is allowing their children to be who they are—instead of trying to make them into who they think they "should" be. I see this play out in family dynamics repeatedly, particularly when it comes to school and the pressure to compete. This requires us to let go of and grieve the loss of the expectations we have of our children, and just allow them to "be."

Being a parent is no easy feat. Once you combine parenting styles with a child's desire to develop their own thoughts, opinions, and ways of doing things—"boom!" You have an interesting situation on your hands. My feeling is that parents are present to help guide children, not dictate to them. To support them, not give orders to them. And depending on age, it is a parent's job to empower their children—not make choices for them. As children, we go through the individuation process with our parents several times at different ages. Individuation refers to our ability to learn to decipher where our parents' beliefs and individuality end and where our own beliefs as an individual begin. We see this happen at various stages such as when we first learn to walk, go off to school, become teenagers, start driving, attend college, and when we move out on our own. Each of these stages is a time of assessment for parents and children. During this time, parents need to evaluate the limits they have set in place. Has their child earned new freedoms?

Are there new choices that the child can begin to make on their own?

This assessment is vital in a parent's ability to see their children as individuals and encourage them accordingly. All children have varying needs and maturity levels, which have an effect on this process.

These stages can trigger different emotions that may prove more uncomfortable than anticipated for both parties. As a child takes on their own independence and belief systems, we may agree with some of their newfound modes of thinking and behaving—and disagree with others. As a parent, how we process and respond to each of these stages of growth makes all the difference in the world.

Over the years of providing individual and family therapy with adolescents, I see how clearly each child just wants to be seen and heard by their parents, and within the family system. What happens when they don't feel seen or heard? Parents begin to see their children behaving differently—not necessarily good or bad, just different—and then a reaction ensues. When we see children acting differently, it is essential that we become curious instead of reactive. This is necessary whether we are a parent, teacher, counselor, therapist, coach, or anyone in their life.

For many, the initial reaction is to get angry or worried, create limits, and find a teachable moment as we fear what is happening might not be reasonable or acceptable. As I have referenced before, our reaction is where our power lies.

We need to give children the ability to "play" with their ideas and choices. We should give them the space to discuss their desires—as crazy as they may sound. What's the harm in listening?

Home is where we should be able to experiment with thoughts, ideas, and emotions; it is a parent's job to create the safe space for this to happen. If the adults in a child's life become so anxious about everything that comes out of their mouth, then reflexively, out of fear, we become more restrictive. This teaches children nothing other than to rebel in their own way. Outward defiance, control with food, perfectionism, and the like can then show up, which complicates matters further.

Years ago, I worked with the parents of a sixteen-year-old girl named Suzie. They were worried that Suzie was struggling with a great deal of anxiety and they felt she was withdrawn socially. When Suzie came into my office for the first time, she was shy, reserved, and well spoken. Her eyes would travel up to look at me and then quickly back down to the floor for most of the session.

After a few weeks of coming to session, Suzie began to appear more comfortable and would speak more freely. Over time, she expressed how her older sister was "really pretty, smart, funny, and everyone likes her" while her younger brother is "so kind, popular, and cute." When I would ask her, "Where do you feel you belong?" she would say, "I don't know."

Initially, we spent the sessions exploring what she enjoys and made her feel good. We also discussed what she felt she was good at and her favorite traits about herself. We then began to look at her family dynamic, and her role within it. As we dug deeper, we were able to see that, due to the fact that she was a quieter child, she would very easily get "lost in the sauce" at home as her siblings took up more space. She would often compare herself to them, and since she didn't feel she was "good enough" at any one thing, she felt she was better off remaining in the background. The more she withdrew, the more her parents would get anxious and try to force her to play with friends, engage in sports that she didn't like, and have her evaluated by multiple professionals in order to see what was wrong with her.

As a result, we were able to see how the role of disappearing into the background reinforced that she didn't feel seen or heard by anyone. She had expressed that when she tried to speak up for her needs to her parents, they would brush her off and say, "Oh, honey, you'll be fine," or "You're being too sensitive; you need to let it go." After this epiphany, we were able to discuss that the therapy office was her space to start practicing with the way in which she wanted to show up in the world. We explored this by discussing scenarios that she encountered at home or at school and role-played the various ways she could express herself. When she came in with a situation she was struggling with regarding her siblings, we would explore how she handled it. We went through how she would like to handle it in the future, and what changes in approach she is comfortable trying.

By exploring her feelings in different scenarios, we were able to see the pattern of her behavior and how she gets in her own way of being seen or heard.

As we continued to work together, we would celebrate her changes and focus on how she was able to put them into play. This helped her feel more confident in her choices by finding ways her needs could be met through healthier measures. At times, with her permission, I would speak with her parents alone to work with them on techniques they could employ at home to support the great work their daughter was doing. My work with her parents was challenging at times as they had some difficulty seeing the role they played in her withdrawal from the family. We would also have her parents come into session in order to work through things that were bothering her, as she didn't quite feel confident enough to address certain issues alone.

As therapists, we walk a fine line in these situations. Sometimes we do it well, and sometimes we don't. In this particular situation, awareness was what was required. It wasn't about blame or that anyone had done anything wrong; it was only about helping her family see and understand Suzie's perception—and how to honor that at home. This is even more important when children are faced with divorced parents. It is essential for parents to come together in support of their children at that juncture, regardless of any other family dynamics.

***In what ways can you empower the children in your life, whether they are your own or someone else's?***

*Chapter Eighteen*

## Chapter Nineteen

**MAINTAINING KINDNESS THROUGH A DIVORCE**

Why is it so hard to maintain kindness through the divorce process? When we find ourselves in the midst of a divorce, whether we are the one that filed for divorce or we are the recipient of divorce papers, we tend to forget why we loved this person in the first place. We become utterly riddled with anger, sadness, grief, and the despair of how our plan for life has completely deviated off course. Within this new reality, all of our past hurt and pain tend to surface, and we hold onto all of it for dear life in order to get through the process. However, what we really need to do is remember the good things about the person we vowed to spend the rest of our lives with. It is the love we felt when we met our partner that is essential to access.

Is that even possible?

Tapping into that love is crucial. If we come from a place of pain and anger, the people that suffer are our families and ourselves. Children learn how to interact with the world around them by observing the examples set by their parents.

As mentioned in an earlier chapter, we learn how to treat the opposite sex when we recall how our parents treated each other. When we come from a place of anger as a result of hurt or sadness, we are deceiving ourselves if we think it will be a helpful way to drudge through the divorce process. We also show our loved ones the "ugly" side of our pain instead of the healthy way to work through something scary and difficult.

***Take some time here to explore ways in which you struggle to let go of anger in order to move forward.***

## *Children of Divorce*

Children need healthy parents in their lives. To me, there is no question about this. As a couple, whether we are heterosexual, two fathers, or two mothers, we provide a balance to our children's lives that can't be replaced by a single parent—regardless of how good we think we are. However, it's not easy to make room for someone in your child's life toward whom you feel varying degrees of animosity. It may be difficult to remember when we are hurting, but there was a point when we considered our partner to be a wonderful companion and potential parent. Isn't that why we chose to be with them?

Why is it that people forget that fact during a divorce? It doesn't have to be that way.

## *Where to start? Ask yourself the following:*

Are there traits of your soon-to-be-ex-spouse that align with yours?

What are the morals and values you both share that you wish to pass on to your children?

Children learn by actions, not words. Your words mean nothing if they see your actions contradict your words on a daily basis. Your ability to rise above your anger and tune into your pain is what will get you through the process in a more humanistic and compassionate way. Everyone's life in a family system is disrupted by divorce; you are not the only one suffering and trying to figure out "what the hell am I supposed to do now?" Take a minute each day and reflect on what you have learned from your marriage and the divorce process. Each partner has played a role in why the marriage has ended up where it is at this juncture. It is key to be able to take a step back and acknowledge the role you played and how you can do things differently moving forward.

None of us is perfect, and we need to remember this when we are trying to work with our ex-spouse to provide the best possible life we can for our children. If you don't access your pain, you are denying yourself the ability to heal. You are also depriving your children of the opportunity to understand what it means to rise above adversity and adapt to change in a healthy way.

***How do you avoid dealing with pain and how does this prevent you from working together with someone who has hurt you?***

## *Decisions of Divorce*

I've read so many articles about "the best way" to co-parent and I work with people around co-parenting issues. What it all boils down to is this: there is no perfect way to navigate divorce, and that's something we all need to accept. When it comes to supporting children of divorce, we need to acknowledge that they view and internalize divorce in completely different ways. Please stop trying to look for the "perfect" answer as to how to co-parent or support children of a divorce. *Just stop and listen to them.* In their purest form, children simply want their parents to stop arguing, get along, and to love them. We all know that each child has different needs, and it is our job to discern how to meet these needs.

I had an eye-opening moment the other day with my son. I think it's important to share, in order to provide insight if you have a child in your life who is struggling with the effects of separation or divorce. Although similar to the episode I had with him about band practice, this time was different as it opened my eyes to what goes through the mind of a child of divorced parents.

He was dragging his feet to get ready to leave the house, which is unusual for him. We were running a little behind, and at one point, my son started crying and went to his room to get back in bed. I went in and said, "What's wrong?" He looked at me and replied, "I don't want to go to school, and I don't like school! I just want to stay home."

I replied, "Honey, not today. Let's finish getting ready." So he continued to get ready, and each step of the way felt like pulling teeth.

When we got into the car to head up to the bus stop, he began crying again and this time it was a bigger cry. He looked at me with tears streaming down his face and said, "I have no time. I have no time to feel and express my emotions, and I just have no time!" In the moment, I had to quickly assess and consider how I was going to handle this. If he missed the bus then I would have to drive him and I had meetings all day. This would put me seriously behind schedule.

Then I had a "come to Jesus" moment with myself. I made the decision that no matter what was going to happen or how severely I was going to mess up my work schedule, I was going to function out of what's best for him—and not react out of stress.

He was really crying by this point. The bus pulled up and I waved it to go on, as I had decided to drive him to school. This was the best decision I could have ever made.

I want to acknowledge at this point that I am very fortunate that my son is extremely intuitive and has exceptional emotional intelligence for a nine-year-old boy (yes, I am very biased). We left the bus stop and pulled down into the driveway and he said, "Mom, I feel like I have too many decisions to make—and it's so stressful and there is so much pressure." For context, the day before, our neighbors had invited him to play at their house after school. But he had already committed to go to his father's for the night so they could watch a television episode that they enjoy. I asked him, "What decisions are you referring to?" and he replied, "All of them. It would just be easier if you and Dad lived together because there are things that I really like about being with Dad and there are things that I really like about being with you." He then went on to express how dissimilar the two households were and how different his father and his stepmother were from my husband and me. I sat and listened as I thought to myself, *What a gift I have been given to have a son who is able to so clearly express himself and his feelings.* This thought was followed by, *OK, you have this gift so don't say too much, just listen.* And that's what I did. I listened, and I was curious.

As a parent in these moments, it can be very hard not to take things personally or get defensive. At our core, we just feel awful that someone we love so dearly is in pain and that we have played a role in why he has to experience these emotions—as his life has taken a dramatic turn. Yes, it's tough to be quiet and listen when the air is filled with pain. But that's OK.

At one point during our conversation I asked him, "Would it help if Dad and I made some of these decisions for you?" He quietly replied, "No. Because no matter who makes the decision, I am still missing out on something." At that point, with tears flowing down my face, I looked at him and said, "Honey, I'm sorry," as I leaned over to hold him tightly. We both sat in the front seat of my car, crying, hugging, and crying some more. It was truly one of the most beautiful moments of my life.

We were able to share in the pain instead of avoiding it and letting it linger. After a few minutes of this—and verbalizing how grateful we are for each other—my son looked over at me and said, "We should probably get going, Mom. I don't want to be late for school." So I wiped my eyes, gave him a kiss, and off we went.

What I have learned from my sons, through our blended family, is that they are begging for us to hear and honor how hard divorce is for them. I am so tired of people saying, "Kids are resilient; they will be fine." I feel like that is a way to minimize human emotions—and that doesn't sit well with me. Yes, they are resilient, but that doesn't mean that they don't experience the depths of emotions that we do. And why do we expect them to do things or deal with things that we as adults wouldn't tolerate or allow in our relationships? What are we teaching them by having this double standard? I think it's wrong.

We need to open the space for our kids, or anyone for that matter, to say the uncomfortable and to speak their pain. That's how we will play a major role in their ability to listen and trust their intuition. Not everything is a teachable moment: the teachable moment is when we truly listen.

Our best teachable moments are also when we aren't saying anything and our children are simply observing our behavior and our interactions. In our household, we are clear with our children that, as long as they are respectful, they are allowed to express when they disagree or feel something isn't right. The beauty in this is that it gives them the space to find their voice and advocate for themselves in an appropriate way. When they are out in the world, this is a skill they have developed that they have already practiced at home. If you think about it, whether we are the children growing up or we are the parents raising children, our home is our practicing ground for how we want to be in the real world. If home is a place where we can't express our true selves, then how will we know how to show up authentically in our relationships outside of our home?

That's right, we won't.

## *Action Step*

It's this simple—when your child or loved one is talking, just listen. Be curious. Stop teaching, stop trying to fix, and stop trying to have an answer for everything. Just listen.

## *What prevents you from listening when children speak?*

## LEADERSHIP AND FAMILY SYSTEMS DYNAMICS

How does one create respect? They listen, and, as a team, encourage collaboration and problem-solving. They also trust their gut instinct. They are confident and able to make decisions and hold themselves accountable. As a result, effective leaders are able to hold others accountable. They show gratitude for the people they work with, knowing that if it weren't for them they may not have a successful business. A good leader also knows how to care for themselves in order to show up as their best self on a regular basis. They are consistent and know how to kindly quash gossip and drama. They understand that people are human beings and are able to define boundaries. At the same time, the best leaders know how to give someone the space to function within the boundaries provided, without micromanaging. A good leader is always interested in how people learn and they possess the ability to ask their employees what they need, without ego.

A leader in an organization functions very much like a leader within a family. If you look closely at family systems theory, there are commonalities that exist. For instance, when you make a change in any family system or business, it will affect the entire dynamic of that system. Time is required for the system to readjust to what's been added or taken away, similar to divorce or death. Another way in which a business resembles a family system is how the balance of power plays out.

When a system changes, if the people within the system trust those in power (or their parents), they are able to get through the shift in a more productive way without fear—knowing they will be cared for. Yet in a business, when someone gets hired or fired, a knee-jerk reaction of insecurity shows up and spreads throughout the organization. When leadership is not respected or trusted, staff members may feel as though they are next on the chopping block. It is this fear that some leaders believe is the impetus for their support staff to function optimally, when in reality it leads to increased burnout and wasted money and resources spent on training new hires at a more frequent pace. In contrast to this belief, employees aren't functioning at their best, which translates into lost revenue over time. The reality is that the leader, piloting a fear-driven team, is actually riddled with fear themselves. This, in turn, becomes projected onto their employees. They are living with their own fear of being worthy, and the fear of competition, of someone taking their position and of their worth going unnoticed.

If you think about it, the same concept applies in a family system. When parents function and make decisions based on fear, they are instilling that fear within their children, which creates anxiety. This, in turn, fuels micromanaging and a feeling of suffocation.

When a leader or parent is able to take time to sit with themselves and understand their own needs, they are better able to discern what emotional baggage is theirs and what belongs to the ones they are interacting with. The fear in parenting and leadership can come from a place of, "How do I allow someone to be creative and free enough to be themselves while still respecting the boundaries of this system?"

Most often, people fear freedom due to a misguided notion that if someone experiences it, in any sense of the word, they will leave and not come back. Of course, the opposite is true. When you allow someone to gain and maintain a sense of freedom, they want to stay where they are because it fulfills them in a way they know they may not find elsewhere. They are able to feel accepted, respected, and at peace with who they are.

## *Action Step for Fear-Based Leadership*

An employee or your child comes to you and says they have made a huge mistake. They become emotional or begin crying and show a great deal of remorse for the choice they made. Your action step as a leader is to sit with them and ask them, "What do you need?" If they are unable to state their need, your follow-up question is, "What do you see as the way to address this situation?" By sitting with them without reaction and asking them these pointed questions, you are allowing space for them to feel, without shame or embarrassment. You are also giving them the space to explore their needs and encouraging them to look at how to be resilient in addressing the issue at hand. It is a solution-based focus that circumvents stewing in self-blame.

***Try the action step above and then take time to journal below how that felt.***

# Chapter Twenty-One

## CONGRUENCE WITH SELF AND OTHERS IN THE WORKPLACE

I have been very fortunate in my career and have experienced wonderful growth opportunities that at times have also come with pain. The challenges I faced were predicated on this feeling that my ability to be decisive, handle crises, and "take the bull by the horns" was the determining factor as to why I was hired for leadership positions. Yet the same skills have been used against me when I wasn't "conforming."

In our society, there are extremely mixed messages for people in positions of power. The message can be "I want you to take care of this stuff so I don't have to" and then, when it is taken care of, the narrative becomes, "That's not the way I wanted it done."

I tend to see this issue occurring more so in women—particularly women working in corporate settings. This "tough girl" skill is developed at a young age to protect themselves emotionally from the world around them. Some have been taught—or their environment has reinforced—that *if I show emotion it is seen as weakness and therefore will be used against me.* This is the complete opposite of emotional safety. As many of these young girls grow into women and step into the world—often in leadership positions—they are given mixed messages about how they are expected to show up. I have experienced this firsthand.

I have always approached leadership based on the premise that my team and I determine goals or the job at hand that needs to be completed together. I would go over parameters and we explore thoughts collectively as to how the job would be most effectively executed. Typically, when a staff member came to me with a challenge or issue, the first thing I'd say is, "What do you think needs to happen?" Or "How do you think this needs to be handled?" I feel very strongly that when we hire people we trust to do a job, it follows that we should give them the space to do what they need to do. My recurring quote is, "You know you need to get from point A to point B; how you choose to do it within the bounds that we have outlined is your choice." This is the freedom I have experienced in certain positions—and the freedom that has been taken from me in others.

So, what does congruence with self and the world around us have to do with this? Well, it has to do with our ability as human beings to be honest with ourselves and as a result make our choices moving forward. It is our responsibility to understand how we show up in the world and then engage in a "gut check" to ensure that our choices feel right for who we are.

## *Action Step*

Try asking a few people in your life who will give you kind feedback—and people you trust to be honest. Ask them what they see when they look at you. How would they describe you to someone else? Share with them that you are working on the aspect of congruence. Once you have feedback from them, take some time to sit with how you are perceived by others. Notice which points have validity and which feel as though they do not fit (this is where you can hone your intuition). Very often, how we perceive ourselves and how others perceive us can be different in certain ways.

Ask yourself, "Is how I am perceived in line with who I am?" and write down your answers. If these observations are not reflective of who you are, then how do you need to behave in order for them to be reflected to the world differently?

Make lists. They will act as a reference and keep you on track.

***Notes:***

# Chapter Twenty-Two

## DO YOU HAVE DATA TO BACK THAT UP?

As technology and science continues to reach new heights, I have seen our society retreat further and further into our head (assessing everything through logic and reason) and out of our heart (feeling and hearing our intuition). Why is this important to note? All over the United States, mental health treatment facilities use the phrase "we provide evidence-based treatment" to help assure prospective patients that the tools they use are justified and effective. It is that simple statement that allows the majority of people trying to navigate the system of mental health to think, *Well then, it must be good treatment if they have data to back it up.*

Yes, numbers and data can be helpful to establish patterns and theories, but they certainly do not represent the entire picture. We need to take other things into account, such as the type of person we are working with—and look at them as a whole, not just at pieces of them. We need to take into account whether or not the therapeutic approach is further reinforcing someone to be in their head (thinking and analyzing) instead of in their heart (feeling). How are we able to help people feel when we are continually having them *think* about their feelings or analyzing their feelings instead of just sitting with them *in their feelings*?

Psychotherapy is a wonderful way to start this process. Then there is the next layer, which looks different for everyone. As we know, there is no "one fix" that works for everyone. I am convinced that we need to look at what the process for each individual is in order to help them explore their body in addition to their thoughts. What this means is that, for certain individuals, some experiential therapies resonate more than others. For some, art therapy is extremely effective. For others it's Reiki, and for others it may be acupuncture. At the end of the day, it revolves around what feels best to clients and what steps they are willing to take. This requires attunement from the therapist to be able to acknowledge when therapy has reached a plateau and to explore experiential methods of healing with clients in ways that feel right for them. We have lost sight of our ability to discern what feels right—and what feels off—by thinking that since there is "data to back it up," it must be right.

If you reflect back over the years you have been alive, at one point the data supported that chocolate was bad for you. Then years later, new data came out stating that dark chocolate was actually good for you. This is one example of the many variables constantly at play for all of us as human beings. There is no way to have hard and fast data when no two people are exactly the same.

Years ago, when I was employed by various treatment facilities, I was working with a man in order to admit him for treatment. He was diagnosed with bipolar disorder and had been off his medication for a period of time prior to admission. During the admission process, he became anxious, agitated, and fearful that we would overmedicate him and send him on his way, as other treatment facilities had done in the past. I took some time to assure him that we would work closely with him to avoid the frustration and fear that he felt in the past to achieve a different experience for him. As this gentleman went through the process, I received multiple phone calls from different providers on the treatment team that he was delusional and showing psychotic tendencies, indicating that he may need inpatient stabilization. The treatment team feared we were not equipped to do this as we were a residential treatment facility and did not provide acute stabilization. I had jumped into several meetings with this client and the providers he was meeting with for initial evaluations, and saw that his paranoia was truly valid. He was in a state of trauma response.

After he had struggled throughout the day, we met as an entire treatment team to figure out what the best course of action would be to protect the patient, the residential community, and our staff. We decided after lengthy discussions that this young man needed us to sit with him in this moment and not send him off. We needed to earn his trust and not repeat the cycle of trauma, which further disrupted his healing and his ability to find the appropriate medication regimen.

I'm so grateful I was able to be part of that decision-making process, as this young man went on to be extremely successful throughout his stay in residential treatment. He was also able to find a medication regimen that worked for him. The moral of this story is that we could have had the best treatment facility in the world with data to back up our treatment modalities but in the end, if we didn't work to gain this patient's trust, none of this would have taken place. The situation required patience, kindness, and our ability as providers to look beyond the diagnosis. We needed to sit with the human being right in front of us who was terrified that he would have the same experience he'd had in the past. He needed to know that we would not simply discard him as his diagnosis, and instead, treat him as a human being.

### *Action Step*

If you are in a situation where you or a loved one need to seek therapeutic help, whether it be on an outpatient basis once a week or staying at a facility, take the time to write down first impressions as soon as you get off the phone with a potential treatment provider. Write down how it felt engaging with the person during the admissions process. If your stomach turns and you feel as though you are being fed a line of BS, trust it. If you get off the phone and feel as though you connected with the person you were talking to, trust it. Don't overthink—easier said than done—*just feel*.

**Utilize this action step and write below how it felt when reaching out to a new doctor, making a new friend, or interviewing a new employee.**

# Addendum

## *Nutrition and the Mind-Body Connection*

We are living in a time when it is reinforced that "all organic" is the best way to go, and yet, how many people can actually afford to purchase solely organic foods? When our parents were growing up—at least those in the 1920s, '30s, and '40s—everything was organic by nature. It wasn't until corn syrup and other substitutes came onto the scene that we adopted the "all organic" marketing tool to make more money and mass-produce. Due to these additives and fillers, our bodies are receiving things that aren't good for us and are foreign in nature. Corn syrup and other additives are mysteriously concealed within the ingredients of myriad products and very often we don't even know how to decipher what is actually in the foods we are eating. The current sage advice is to grocery-shop around the perimeter of the store, which is a good practice. Food is our body's source of fuel and energy.

The problem is that people have become so obsessed with this that we are teaching people to be out of balance as we impress upon them to only eat a certain way. In "strong-arming" our loved ones to only consume specific foods, we are creating a theme of good vs. bad and not nurturing a philosophy of balance. The inherent goal in eating is to help someone determine how they feel in their body after they eat certain foods, in order to identify which foods make them feel well and which foods make them feel poorly. This is the perfect opportunity to take the time to feel how our body is affected by what we put into it. Creating the space for our family to do this requires mealtime to be sacred, calm, and without distraction. Is this possible every single day? No, not necessarily, but if this is more consistent than not, it is a great start.

Recently, I had to have my gallbladder removed. My surgeon said that there was about twenty years' worth of damage and inflammation and a gallstone the size of a gumball to boot. I asked her, "Why hasn't any one of my doctors suggested having an ultrasound of my gallbladder over the years if it is that diseased?" Her reply was, "You don't fit the profile," to which I responded, "You can't judge a book by its cover." People talk about having their gallbladder removed as if they just pulled out a splinter, when in reality, your gallbladder serves a solid function in your digestive system in breaking down the fats you eat. How would one know this? I sure didn't. I was sad that it had to go as I would prefer to keep all of my body parts, and yet now that it's out I feel like a new woman. I have struggled with GI issues my whole life, in part due to what I chose to eat—and the frequency with which I ate it. Then, of course, there's genetics—and I can't deny that there was also an aspect of where my emotions were stored in my body. When I met my husband, he opened my eyes to the way in which food sensitivities play a major role in the functioning of our body. It wasn't until I was in my forties that I learned that what I was eating was causing an intense reaction in my body, which exacerbated my GI issues immensely. I have seen GI doctors for the better part of twenty years and never once was I encouraged to complete food sensitivity testing to see if what I was eating was creating inflammation.

After completing the food sensitivity tests and altering some of the highest offenders in my diet, I started to feel incredible relief from my GI system issues. I took the inflammatory foods out, learned how to read labels, and then reintroduced the "problem" foods in a way that my body could handle, without being reactive. Did I need to struggle for twenty years with pain from acid reflux? The answer is I didn't; however, you don't know what you don't know. A huge part of my diet and GI issues was the result of only eating foods I liked and then eating them all the time, which was too much for my system to handle. But it baffles me that no one took the time to explore what I was eating and how that made my body feel. This saddens me.

Our medical system has transformed into Band-Aid solutions. Doctors often throw medications at things so we have the illusion of healing, yet all we are doing is masking the issue on a physical, emotional, and spiritual level. We need to feel how our food sits in our body—whether eating cheese creates sinus congestion or eating red meat creates pain in our lower intestines. This is what's important, not which proton pump inhibitor will make the reflux go away.

Did people tell me years ago to stop eating Reese's Pieces? Yes. Did I listen? No. At that time I wasn't able to hear the message that was being communicated. This is where balance comes in. Anyone you speak to with wisdom will share their reflection of life with you. The adage "don't deprive yourself of the 'sweetness' life has to offer" rings true. I believe in that wholeheartedly and I also believe that it requires balance and not abuse. The best gift we can give our loved ones—and ourselves—is to look at the beauty in healing ourselves. When something is wrong with our bodies, we need to honor that and try to heal it.

I had abused foods for so long that my body was in a reactive state all the time, which stopped me from truly feeling how different foods affected me.

Thanks to the support of my husband, this is no longer the case, and it has been life changing for me. Our bodies are finely tuned and extremely individualized. We do not fit into a one-size-fits-all bucket. In order to find balance it is important to be open to seeking care and the solutions that feel best to you. Be willing and open to exploring natural and alternative ways of healing.

For example, take probiotics; they are a beautiful thing. Yet did you know that each person requires different probiotics for their GI system to function optimally? Unfortunately, this is not something most people are aware of, and as a result they may be taking something that their bodies do not need; they may be doing more harm than good. We know we are all unique in our emotions, thoughts, and spirits, so why aren't we similarly supported when it comes to our bodies and medical care?

## *Action Step*

Think about your favorite foods. Are these foods being consumed in a balanced manner—regardless of whether you deem them "healthy" or not? If the answer is "no," then think about how you can change it up throughout the week. Try this for a few weeks, and then see if you feel a difference in your body. You may feel less lethargic, sleep better at night (particularly if any of these foods contain caffeine), or you may experience more clarity when making decisions. In a sense, food is just like clothing; we can all fall subject to wearing our favorites over and over, ignoring the fabulous new shirt we have in our closet with the tags still attached.

## *Fueling Our Bodies and the Connection to Self-Image*

This is quite a delicate topic. It has become more and more of a "thing" as social media has altered our body image and relationship with food in a wildly negative way. Is it the sole cause?

Not entirely—but it has a great deal of influence on how we view ourselves.

As I meet with clients of all ages and discuss their relationship with food, there are a lot of commonalities I observe. Therapists, doctors, and nutritionists can be extremely apprehensive to work with someone with an eating disorder—or what is often called "disordered eating." They worry that outpatient care may not be enough and they are very concerned about the liability they face if the client's weight is too low. As a result, many professionals will approach the eating disorder in a way that actually fuels the fire instead of forging a path to recovery. Some time ago, a client that I have treated developed a disordered relationship with food. Prior to coming into my care, my client began seeing her pediatrician. He was weighing her weekly and made it clear that in order for her to play the sport she loves she needed to "gain a few pounds." The doctor continued to monitor her weight throughout the period she participated in her beloved sport. I can empathize with the reality of a child being in a healthy weight range, and this child is. As a result of this approach, my client used unhealthy skills prior to her doctor visits purely to "shut the doctor up" and make weight so she could move on.

What many health professionals don't realize is that disordered eating is not about the food; the food is just a symptom of a bigger issue. The more predominant problem is typically an underlying emotional discomfort or emotional dysregulation. It isn't until we look at the underlying issue—and address it—that we are able to truly effect change. I feel that we as practitioners also have to remember that each case is different. We can't only focus on one area of a patient's strained relationship with food; we also need to look at the root cause, which is the emotions that they are trying to avoid. How does their unhealthy relationship with food help them to stay out of their body? What does being healthy look like? How was food talked about as they were growing up? All of these questions are key to gaining a better understanding of why someone's relationship with food has become unhealthy. As the long-established saying goes, the words we use matter. We see this in households around the world in how people speak about food. We often hear the phrase "oh, that's crap." Or, "If I eat this, I will see it on my thighs tomorrow." The phrases change depending on the household. Some homes are numerically driven by what the scale says, while other homes completely banish "sugary" foods. This is yet another example of how we carry forward our parents' belief systems or self-talk, long after we leave their home. When we are raised in a home that talks about food by implying that it's "good" or "bad," we set up a very black-and-white view of everything we eat. At the end of the day, it is the emotion that we correlate with food that matters as well as the respect that we show our bodies. The ideal is to be able to *feel* how your body responds to what you put into it.

Your body will tell you whether it has a positive impact (evidenced by feeling alert and energized) or sensitivity to the food (as evidenced by a stuffy nose, stomach or bowel discomfort, fatigue, headache). The ability to notice these cues requires us to take one step at a time. It requires us to eat a meal and take time to feel our body and notice if anything has shifted afterwards.

Every household needs to be aware of the language they use in regard to weight, food, and health.

Unfortunately, I have seen the discussion of health take very disruptive turns. Being healthy does not mean you deprive yourself of everything and only eat salad. It does not mean that you never have chocolate or you don't enjoy waffles once in a while. Those desires are natural and need to be acknowledged in order for you to develop a healthy relationship with food. Diets don't work. Overexercising does not make one healthy.

Life is about balance and honoring all parts of yourself and your body. It's about listening to your body and feeling the effects of the choices you make.

## *Action Step*

Each time you eat, ask yourself, "Why am I eating right now?" Log your answers in a journal or notepad. The goal is to get you to stop in the moment and tune in to your body, and then determine if you are eating because you are truly hungry—or are you just bored, anxious, or sad? After doing this for a few days and taking mental or physical notes, you can look at the pattern you are engaging in and whether or not you are eating as a result of your hunger or because of an emotion.

### *Notes:*

*Addendum*

# About the author

Throughout her career, Jessica Raistrick has worked with clients in various settings through direct care and leadership positions. She has effectively directed admissions teams, focusing on building and training staff to help families and clients facilitate receiving the critical treatment they require. As her desire to empower her patients and alleviate their mental and physical discomfort deepened, she became certified as a Reiki master. She offers the option for this ancient healing modality in her sessions, to help clients more clearly access their intuition and emotions.

Made in the USA
Middletown, DE
08 June 2025